MISTAKES
THAT WORKED

MISTAKES
THAT WORKED

CHARLOTTE FOLTZ JONES

Illustrated by John O'Brien

DOUBLEDAY

New York / London / Toronto / Sydney / Auckland

PUBLISHED BY DOUBLEDAY
a division of Bantam Doubleday Dell Publishing Group, Inc.
666 Fifth Avenue, New York, New York 10103

DOUBLEDAY
and the portrayal of an anchor with a dolphin
are trademarks of Doubleday, a division of
Bantam Doubleday Dell Publishing Group, Inc.

Library of Congress Cataloging-in-Publication Data
Jones, Charlotte Foltz.
Mistakes that worked / by Charlotte Foltz Jones ; illustrated by
John O'Brien. — 1st ed.
p.   cm.
Includes bibliographical references.
Summary: Presents the stories behind forty things that were
invented or named by accident, including aspirin, X-rays, frisbees,
silly putty, and velcro.
1. Inventions—Juvenile literature. [1. Inventions.]
I. O'Brien, John, 1953- ill. II. Title.
T48.J66 1991
609—dc20
89-37408 CIP AC
ISBN 0-385-26246-9
RL:3.5

DEDICATED TO

FORREST FOLTZ

With Special Thanks to Bill Jones and John Jones

ACKNOWLEDGMENTS

Bangor Chamber of Commerce
Ed Bartley, Dunkin' Donuts
Joan Beliveau, Dunkin' Donuts
Kathie Bellamy, Baskin-Robbins, USA
Barbara and Bill Brownlee, International
  Brick Collectors Association
Mary Cash
Donald A. Fischer, 3M
Claire Jackson, Coca-Cola USA
Betty M. James, James Industries
Patricia M. Jent, Procter & Gamble Co.
Maxine C. Johnson, Scott Paper Co.
Edward Jones, Circus Historical Society
Peggy V. Jue, Levi Strauss & Co.
D'Ann King-Monroe, Tennessee State
  Library and Archives
Corinne Kirchner, American Foundation
  for the Blind
Leoma B. Maxwell, Avon Park Historical
  Society and Museum
Bill McCarthy, Circus World Museum
Sally Miller, Procter & Gamble Co.

Nestlé Foods
Neil Nix, Glenbrook Laboratories, Div.
  Sterling Drug
Nome Convention and Visitors Bureau
John Perduyn, Goodyear Tire & Rubber
  Co.
Potato Chip/Snack Food Association
Roy Renfrow, Malvern Chamber of
  Commerce
Anne Reynolds
Phil Rice
Marvene Riis, South Dakota Historical
  Society
Dan Roddick, Wham-O
Dean Rodenbough, Binney & Smith
Jim Russell, Popsicle Industries
B. E. Saffer, General Shale Museum of
  Ancient Brick
Lori Scholz, The Seeing Eye, Inc.
Harold Sloan
Rob Smelstor, VELCRO, USA
Lina Striglia, Binney & Smith

INTRODUCTION

"Name the greatest of all the inventors. Accident."
Mark Twain (Notebook)

Call them accidents. Call them mistakes. Even serendipity.

If the truth were known, we might be amazed by the number of great inventions and discoveries that were accidental, unplanned and unintentional.

The inventors mentioned in this book were not only smart, but also alert. It is easy to fail and then abandon the whole idea. It's more difficult to fail, but then recognize another use for the failure.

Much research and documentation has gone into each entry of this book, and some fun, interesting, and sometimes humorous stories about various discoveries emerged. Some of the stories are historical fact. Others are legends or lore—stories that cannot be proved and probably can't be disproved.

The discoveries related in this book are just the beginning of ideas. Research, experimentation, and hard work were needed to develop the subjects into the products we use today.

The inventors and discoverers mentioned in this book should teach all of us the lesson stated best by Bertolt Brecht in 1930: "Intelligence is not to make no mistakes. But quickly to see how to make them good."

CONTENTS

MISTAKES
THAT WORKED

1
TUMMY FILLERS

Many cooks admit their favorite recipes were the result of accidents. But the numerous cases of food poisoning prove many food accidents don't work.

If you would like to experiment in the kitchen, a good book to start with is Vicki Cobb's *Science Experiments You Can Eat* (J. B. Lippincott, New York). But be careful. The National Safety Council reports that almost eight hundred thousand accidents involving home kitchen appliances and housewares are treated in hospital emergency rooms each year. So learn the safety rules and don't become a statistic.

KITCHEN SAFETY TIPS

1. Ask permission from a parent or other adult before beginning any kitchen project.
2. Always wash your hands before handling foods or cooking utensils.
3. Read the recipe carefully and get out all ingredients and equipment before you begin.
4. Follow the recipe exactly and measure accurately.
5. Use electrical appliances only with an adult's supervision.
6. When you are finished, put unused ingredients away and clean the kitchen. Never leave a mess.

Brown 'n Serve Rolls

Baking rolls or bread is not quick.

The ingredients are mixed, then kneaded. The dough rises for one to two hours. Then it gets punched, divided into rolls, and baked for at least another hour.

Joe Gregor *knew* there must be an easier way for busy people to have hot rolls. He spent long hours trying to devise a method, but without success.

Then one afternoon in 1949, Gregor was baking dinner rolls in his Avon Park, Florida, kitchen when the fire siren wailed. As a volunteer fireman, he had to respond to the fire. He quickly pulled the rolls from the oven and rushed out the door.

When he returned from the fire, Gregor examined the cold, half-cooked rolls. They were white and looked like plaster. Most people would have thrown the ugly mess in the garbage. But not Joe Gregor. He reheated his oven and finished cooking the rolls.

They were delicious! Gregor had accidentally discovered a method for making rolls ahead of time, yet serving them hot and fresh at the dinner table.

Gregor experimented to find the exact temperatures and times required for the first baking. He then revealed the directions to bakers everywhere.

Today bakeries do the mixing, kneading, rising, and even part of the baking. Mr. or Ms. N. A. Hurry can buy brown 'n serve rolls, heat them for ten minutes, and eat! . . . thanks to Joe Gregor and the Avon Park volunteer fire department.

Cheese

There he was: an ancient Arabian traveling across the desert with no one for company but a camel with yellow teeth, bad breath, and a bad temper.

At least the fellow had food along. He had poured some milk into a pouch made from a sheep's stomach. During his journey, he opened the pouch and discovered the milk had separated and formed thick masses, which we call curd, and a watery fluid, which we call whey. The Arabian traveler had accidentally invented cheese.

Two elements transformed the milk into cheese: First, the sun warmed the bag of milk during the journey. Second, the sheep-stomach bag contained dried digestive juices. The digestive juices included "rennet," which is necessary to make cheese even today.

The Arabian traveler told his friends about his discovery and for four thousand years people have continued making cheese. Cheese quickly became important all over the world. Milk spoiled quickly, but by making cheese, people could preserve the milk's nutrition for long periods of time.

If you are an average American, you ate 24 pounds of cheese last year. That's what the National Cheese Institute estimates. According to the *Guinness Book of World Records,* while the United States is the largest producer of cheese, the average French person eats the most cheese—43.6 pounds each year.

Over two thousand varieties of cheese are produced around the world. If you tasted a different kind each week, it would take almost forty years to sample all the varieties. And by that time, someone would probably have developed some new ones to try, too.

— According to the *Guinness Book of World Records,* the largest cheese ever made was 40,060 pounds. It was made in 1988 in Wisconsin. A specially designed, refrigerated "cheese-mobile" moved the giant cheese from place to place.
— The American Dairy Association sponsors National Dairy Month during June.
— "Cheese" in other languages is:

French	fromage	Hungarian	sajt
Spanish	queso	Russian	sir
Italian	formaggio	Japanese	chiizu
German	Käse	Swahili	jibini
Polish	ser	Swedish	ost

Chocolate Chip Cookies

George Washington never tasted one.
Neither did Benjamin Franklin, Abraham Lincoln, nor Mark Twain.
Unfortunately, they died before the chocolate chip cookie was invented.
Thanks to Ruth Wakefield, chocolate chip cookies were invented in 1930 and are available all over America today.

Wakefield did not plan to invent a cookie that would become the country's favorite. She was busy with the chores of running the Toll House Inn, located on the toll road between Boston and New Bedford, Massachusetts.

While mixing a batch of cookies, Wakefield discovered she was out of baker's chocolate. As a substitute she broke some semi-sweetened chocolate into small pieces and added them to the dough. She expected the chocolate bits to melt and the dough to absorb them, producing chocolate cookies.

When she removed the pan from the oven, Wakefield was surprised. The chocolate had not melted into the dough, and her cookies were not chocolate cookies. Wakefield had accidentally invented the chocolate chip cookie.

They were named Toll House cookies after Ruth Wakefield's inn and are the most popular variety in America today. Estimates say seven billion chocolate chip cookies are consumed annually, and half the cookies baked in American homes are chocolate chip.

These popular treats have even provided full-time jobs; some vendors sell nothing but chocolate chip cookies.

They also made a political appearance in 1980. After Canadian diplomats assisted six American hostages to escape from Iran, the American people sent chocolate chip cookies to the Canadian embassy—our way of saying "thanks."

If you would like to make chocolate chip cookies, the following recipe is furnished by Nestlé Foods for the original Toll House Cookies:

2 1/4 cups unsifted flour
1 measuring teaspoon baking soda
1 measuring teaspoon salt
1 cup butter, softened
3/4 cup white sugar
3/4 cup firmly packed brown sugar
1 measuring teaspoon vanilla extract
2 eggs
One 12-ounce package (2 cups) Nestlé
*   Semi-Sweet Real Chocolate Morsels*
1 cup chopped nuts

Preheat oven to 375° F. In small bowl, combine flour, baking soda, and salt; set aside. In large bowl, combine butter, white sugar, brown sugar, and vanilla extract; beat

until creamy. Beat in eggs. Gradually add flour mixture; mix well. Stir in chocolate morsels and nuts. Drop by rounded teaspoonfuls onto ungreased cookie sheets.

Bake at 375° F.
Time: 8–10 minutes
Makes one hundred 2″ cookies

Coca-Cola

The date was May 8, 1886.

The Civil War had been over twenty-one years.

Grover Cleveland was President of the United States.

And in Atlanta, Georgia, a pharmacist named John Pemberton was busy in his backyard. Pemberton had already invented "French Wine Coca—The Ideal Nerve Tonic, Health Restorer and Stimulant," "Lemon and Orange Elixir," and "Dr. Pemberton's Indian Queen Magic Hair Dye." But he wanted to invent a remedy for people who imbibed too much.

Using a boat oar to stir, Pemberton cooked up a mixture in a brass kettle heated over an open fire. When he finished, he had a new medicine to relieve exhaustion, aid the nervous, and soothe headaches.

Pemberton took his new medicine to the Jacobs Pharmacy. He instructed Venable, his assistant, to mix the syrup with water and chill it with ice. They tasted it and agreed it was delicious. But when Venable mixed another glass, he accidentally added carbonated water instead of plain water.

This time the men became excited. They decided that instead of offering the beverage as a headache remedy, they would sell it as a fountain drink—an alternative to ginger ale and root beer. They named it Coca-Cola after the coca leaves and cola nuts it contained.

In 1886, Coca-Cola sales averaged nine drinks a day. According to the Coca-Cola Company, Pemberton sold twenty-five gallons of syrup that first year. He took in $50 but spent $73.96 on advertising.

People in 155 countries drink 393 million Coca-Cola soft drinks every day. Pemberton's invention is not famous as a headache remedy or exhaustion relief. Instead it's one of the world's favorite beverages.

— **A private museum in Kentucky exhibits a hundred years of Coca-Cola advertising memorabilia. You can visit it at:**

The Schmidt Coca-Cola Museum
P. O. Box 647
1201 North Dixie Avenue
Elizabethtown, Kentucky 42701
There is an admission charge.

- According to the Coca-Cola Company, if all the Coke ever produced was placed in twelve-ounce cans and stacked in single columns next to Mount Everest, it would take 19 million columns of cans to hold the Coke.
- Today, fourteen of Coca-Cola's ingredients are generally well known, but the fifteenth ingredient is known only as "7X." This mystery ingredient is one of the best-guarded secrets in the country. Only a few people know the true identity of "7X" and they are not allowed to travel together in case of an accident.

Doughnut Holes

Hanson Gregory was born in 1832 in Camden, Maine, and died in 1921. He is buried in the Sailors' Snug Harbor Cemetery in Germantown, Maine. During the eighty-nine years that Hanson Gregory lived, he spent many of them as a sea captain. A legend says that is where he invented the doughnut hole.

One night he was eating a fried cake when a violent storm suddenly arose. Captain Gregory needed both hands to steer the ship so he shoved the cake over one of the spokes of the ship's helm. Without thinking, he invented the doughnut hole.

When Captain Gregory realized what he had invented, he was pleased. The centers of fried cakes were always unpleasantly soggy, so removing the center definitely improved the cakes. After the storm, Captain Gregory ordered the ship's cook to begin making fried cakes with a hole in the middle.

Another less interesting story says that when Gregory was fifteen, he was watching his mother make fried cakes. Since he disliked the soggy centers, he simply suggested she remove them. Mrs. Gregory tried her son's idea and it worked.

Today over $750 million worth of doughnuts are sold each year. That's a lot of doughnut holes!

Teacher: Who invented the hole in the doughnut?
Student: Some fresh air fiend, I suppose.

Fudge

The dictionary's first definition of the word "fudge" is "nonsense or foolishness." And that's how our favorite chocolate candy got its name.

A story says that in the 1890s, a candy-maker in Philadelphia, Pennsylvania, was supervising his employees as they made caramels. Someone made a mistake and instead of producing a chewy candy, the batch turned into a finely crystallized, nonchewy substance.

"Fudge!" the candy-maker swore. And with that exclamation to describe the mistake, fudge was born.

Through the years there have been many variations of fudge, but here is a simple recipe:

CREAM CHEESE FUDGE

1 six-ounce package semi-sweet chocolate morsels
2 three-ounce packages cream cheese, softened
4 cups sifted confectioners' sugar
2 tablespoons evaporated milk
1 1/2 teaspoons vanilla
1/4 teaspoon salt
2 cups chopped nuts

Melt the chocolate morsels in the top of a double boiler. In a mixing bowl, beat cream cheese until smooth. Add confectioners' sugar and evaporated milk. Stir the melted chocolate into the cheese mixture. Add the vanilla and salt, then the chopped nuts. Press mixture into a well-greased 9-inch square pan. Cover and refrigerate overnight.

(Note: Cream Cheese Fudge is a modern recipe and *not* the original "mistake" recipe.)

Ice Cream Cone

The Chinese made iced desserts thousands of years ago, and George Washington was fond of ice cream, but the ice cream cone was not popular until after 1904.

Two food vendors had stands near each other at the 1904 World's Fair in St. Louis, Missouri. Ernest A. Hamwi, a Syrian who had been in the United States a year, was selling zalabia. Zalabia was a wafer-thin Persian waffle. Nearby, another stand was selling ice cream.

Summer in St. Louis is h-o-t, and the ice cream vendor soon ran out of dishes in which to serve his ice cream. Hamwi quickly rolled one of his waffles into a cone shape

and topped it with a scoop of the neighbor's ice cream. The treat was an instant hit and the "World's Fair Cornucopia" became what we know today as the ice cream cone.

While the story of Hamwi's ice cream cone is generally accepted, another man thought a lot like Hamwi. An Italian named Italo Marchiony ran a pushcart business in New York City selling lemon ice in a cone. At first he used a paper cone, then a pastry one.

Marchiony even applied for a patent in September 1903, and received it in December—six months before the St. Louis World's Fair began.

Great minds think alike! Both Hamwi and Marchiony devised the idea for an ice cream cone. But it was probably the large number of people who tasted Hamwi's cones at the St. Louis World's Fair that made the ice cream cone the popular treat we know today.

Maple Syrup

Warm days. Cool nights.

That's the magic formula for sugar maple tree growers. And February through March or April is the magic time to tap the trees. A single maple tree might give from ten to twenty-five gallons of sap, but it takes between thirty-five and fifty gallons of sap to make one gallon of syrup.

The history of maple syrup goes back many centuries, and there is a legend about its discovery.

The story says Chief Woksis, an Iroquois, left the camp one day in early March for a day of hunting. As he left, he pulled his tomahawk from the maple tree where he had hurled it the night before. During the day, sap dripped from the tree into a vessel standing close to the tree trunk.

When evening came, the chief's squaw noticed the "tree-water" (which we call sap) in the vessel. She decided to use the tree-water to prepare supper and save herself a trip to the spring. As it cooked, the sap boiled down into a syrup. When Chief Woksis arrived home, he was delighted with the new maple flavor of his supper.

Native Americans called the sweetener "maple-water" and as early explorers and

settlers arrived in North America, they taught the white man how to process maple syrup.

Modern technology is improving the sap-gathering process as well as the evaporation method. But no one can improve on the natural goodness of real maple syrup.

— **The major maple syrup-producing states are:**

Illinois	**New Hampshire**
Indiana	**New York**
Maine	**Ohio**
Maryland	**Vermont**
Massachusetts	**Wisconsin**
Michigan	

— **The American Maple Museum's address is P. O. Box 81, Croghan, New York 13327.**
— **Exact figures are not available, but it is estimated 1,116,000 gallons of maple syrup is produced in the United States in a good year—a $39,662,640 industry.**
— **Canada is also a major producer of maple syrup and maple sugar.**

Popsicles

On September 7, 1975, the Westside Assembly of God Church in Davenport, Iowa, made a huge iced-pop. The *Guinness Book of World Records* lists their 5,750-pound creation as the largest iced lollipop on a stick. The frozen treat might have been big, but it wasn't a genuine Popsicle since Popsicle is a registered trademark name and is made under a patented formula.

Popsicles were actually invented in 1905 by eleven-year-old Frank Epperson of California—and the invention was accidental.

One day Frank mixed some soda water powder and water, which was a popular drink in those days. He left the mixture on the back porch overnight with his stirring stick still in it. The temperature dropped to a record low that night and the next day Frank Epperson had a stick of frozen soda water to show his friends at school.

Eighteen years later—in 1923—Frank Epperson remembered his frozen soda water mixture and began a business producing Epsicles in seven fruit flavors. The name was later changed to the Popsicle.

One estimate says three million Popsicle frozen treats are sold each year. There are more than thirty different flavors to choose from, but Popsicle Industries says the general flavor favorite through the years has remained "taste-tingling orange."

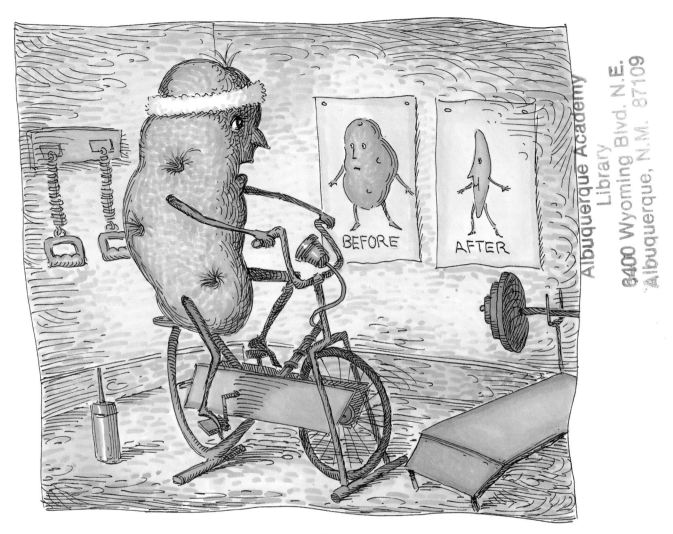

Potato Chips

Americans spend almost $4 billion every year on a treat we know as potato chips. A popular story says they were invented in 1853 in Saratoga Springs, New York. Many wealthy people vacationed at the Carey Moon Lake House in Saratoga Springs and a Native American chef named George Crum worked in the kitchen there.

One day a customer kept sending his plate of fried potatoes back to the kitchen asking that they be sliced thinner and fried longer. George Crum had a bad temper, and he decided to get even with the complaining diner. He sliced the potatoes very thin, fried them till they were curly crisps, and salted them. Certain the guest would hate them, he had the potatoes delivered to the table. To everyone's surprise, the patron was delighted and asked for more.

Word spread quickly of these crispy potatoes and until the early 1900s they were known as Saratoga chips after the town where they were introduced.

Today over 816 million pounds of potato chips are consumed in the United States each year. A total 3.468 billion pounds of potatoes end up as America's number one snack food: potato chips.

— The ordinary, unruffled potato chip is $55/1000$ of an inch thick.
— 11 percent of the total United States potato crop becomes potato chips.
— Charles Chip, Inc. is listed in the *Guinness Book of World Records* as producing the largest potato chip. Displayed in February 1977, it was four inches by seven inches.
— Potato chips are not just potato chips anymore. They are now available in assorted varieties, such as:

cajun	yogurt
jalapeño	barbecue
sour cream with onion	cheese
Italian	cheese with bacon
sour cream	and even chocolate covered!

Sandwiches

The year was 1762.

In America, the Revolutionary War had not yet started, and George Washington was not yet President.

In Europe, six-year-old Wolfgang Amadeus Mozart toured as a child prodigy.

But in England, John Montagu, Fourth Earl of Sandwich, was busy gambling. One

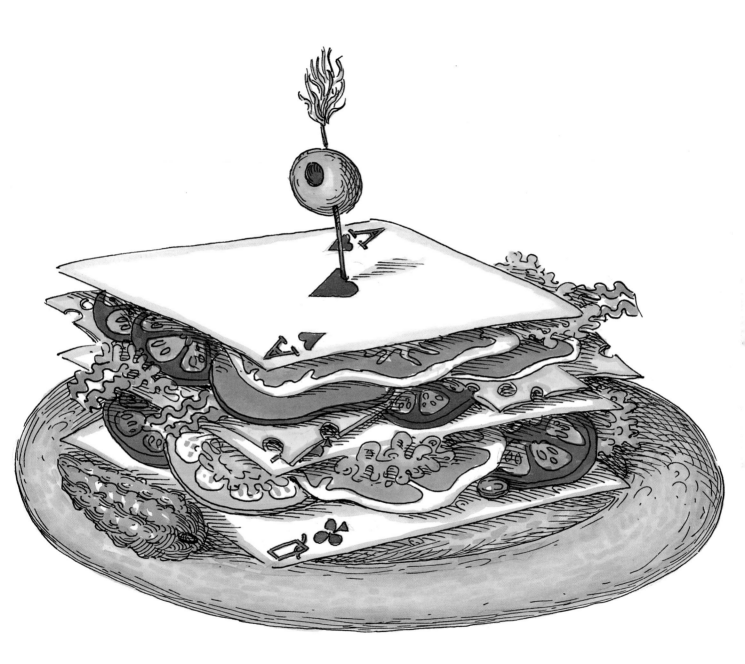

day he had been at the gaming table for twenty-four hours and didn't want to take time out to eat. When the servants brought his food, he ordered the meat served between slices of bread so he could eat and still keep one hand free to control his bets.

And that's how he invented . . . the sandwich.

Bread's history goes back at least six thousand years, so people had probably eaten sandwiches before. But once they were given a famous name, sandwiches became one of the most popular meals eaten in the Western Hemisphere. One estimate says 300 million sandwiches are eaten every day in America.

- **John Montagu was born November 3, 1718, so November 3 is Sandwich Day.**
- **Towns in Illinois and Massachusetts are named Sandwich.**
- **When Captain James Cook discovered the Hawaiian Islands in 1778, he named them the Sandwich Islands in honor of John Montagu.**

Tea

What kind of world would this be without tea?

There would be no teapot or teakettle if tea had never been discovered. There would be no teacup, teaspoon, or tea towel, and no teatime.

Two of the world's most famous parties would have been canceled: The colonists could not have held the Boston Tea Party in 1773, throwing 342 chests of tea into Boston Harbor. And Lewis Carroll's *Alice in Wonderland* would say nothing of the Mad Hatter's and March Hare's tea party.

Luckily, tea was discovered in 2737 B.C. by a great Chinese emperor named Shen Nung.

One day Shen Nung was boiling water outside when leaves from a nearby bush fell into the open kettle. Before Shen Nung could retrieve the leaves, they began to brew. He smelled the sweet aroma of the mixture and once he tasted it, the world was given tea!

Tea is the most popular beverage in the world today—after plain water. It was introduced in Europe in 1610, and until about two hundred years ago, people in many Asian countries used blocks or bricks of tea as money.

One estimate says 2,020,000 metric tons of tea are consumed worldwide each year. That means the people on Planet Earth drink about 855 billion cups of tea a year. That's a lot of tea.

— **13 percent of the world's tea comes from Kenya.**
— **A town in South Dakota is named "Tea."**
— **"Tsiology" is something written about tea.**
— **Around the world, tea is:**

French	**thé**
Spanish	**té**
Turkish	**cay**
Russian	**cháy**
Arabic	**shaye**
Japanese	**cha**

TEA BAGS

Thomas Sullivan invented tea bags, although he did not realize it at the time.

Sullivan, an American coffee and tea merchant, often sent samples of his products to his customers. The samples were packed in cans. One day in 1904, Sullivan decided it would be simpler and less expensive to send the tea samples in small, hand-sewn silk bags.

Soon the orders began arriving, but surprisingly they were not for his tea. The orders were for tea packaged in little bags. The customers had discovered that the small bags made tea brewing easier.

Tea bags have been improved over the years and today over half the tea consumed in American homes is made from them.

2

DOCTOR, DOCTOR

Louis Pasteur, the famous French chemist and bacteriologist, told his students in 1854, "Where observation is concerned, chance favors only the prepared mind."

Aspirin

For thousands of years doctors told patients suffering from pain to chew on the bark of a willow tree. Even as far back as 400 B.C. Hippocrates recommended a tea made from willow leaves.

It wasn't until the 1800s that scientists discovered what was in the willow tree that relieved pain and reduced fever. The substance was named salicylic acid. But when people suffering from pain took the salicylic acid, it caused severe stomach and mouth irritation.

In 1853, a thirty-seven-year-old French chemist named Charles Gerhardt mixed another chemical with the acid and produced good results, but the procedure was difficult and took a lot of time. Gerhardt decided the new compound wasn't practical, so he set it aside.

Forty-one years later a German chemist, Felix Hoffman, was searching for something to relieve his father's arthritis. He studied Gerhardt's experiments and "rediscovered" acetylsalicylic acid—or aspirin, as we now know it.

Charles Gerhardt had mistakenly thought his compound was not useful, but today over 70 million pounds of it are produced annually all over the world.

Scientists are still finding new uses for aspirin. Researchers hope it will prevent heart attacks and strokes, slow the growth of cataracts and cancerous tumors, and help manage diabetes.

Unfortunately, aspirin is not recommended for people under the age of sixteen because of the suspected connection to Reye's syndrome.

Americans take more than 20 billion aspirin tablets a year, making it America's most widely used drug. And the little white tablet is certainly easier to carry in a pocket than the willow tree!

> **Felix Hoffman and his associate Heinrich Dreser gave aspirin its name:**
> **a** — to denote the process of acetylation
> **spir** — because salicylic acid comes from the *spiraea* plant
> **in** — was the fashionable ending for medicines

Dog Guides for Blind People

World War I lasted more than four years—from 1914 to 1918. During that time, approximately 8.5 million people were killed and 21 million were wounded.

Near the end of World War I, a doctor was walking outside a German military hospital with a soldier who had been blinded in battle. The doctor's dog joined the walk and when the doctor was called into one of the buildings, the blind soldier was left alone with the dog.

Soon the doctor returned, but the blind man and the dog were missing. When he found them, he discovered the dog had led the blind patient across the hospital grounds.

The doctor was amazed at what his untrained pet dog had done and decided to see how well a trained working breed of dog could lead a blind person. The results were great and the German government soon expanded the dog guide program.

An American woman named Dorothy Eustis visited Potsdam, Germany, to learn about the dog guide program. Through an article she wrote for *The Saturday Evening Post*, she brought the program to public attention in the United States. The first American dog guide school, The Seeing Eye, Inc., was established in 1929. Today ten major

organizations train dogs and instruct blind people in their use.

The most popular breeds are German shepherds, golden retrievers, and Labrador retrievers. They must learn hand gestures and simple commands in order to lead the blind person across streets and around people, obstacles, holes, and low-hanging awnings or tree limbs.

The dog must also learn to exercise good judgment. If the blind person gives a "forward" command but the dog sees danger, the dog must know when to disobey. This is called "intelligent disobedience."

Dogs guiding blind masters is not new. Wall paintings, ancient scrolls, and legends tell of dogs leading blind men since 100 B.C. But until the German soldier was led by the doctor's untrained dog and the first training program was initiated, the incidents were scattered and the dogs were not always efficient.

In the case of dog guides, the old saying is true: A dog really is a man's—or a woman's—best friend.

— **According to the American Foundation for the Blind, Inc., about 6,500 blind persons in the United States use dog guides.**

Penicillin

Alexander Fleming didn't get out of bed one September morning in 1928 planning to invent penicillin. But that's exactly what he did.

Fleming, then forty-seven years old, was a bacteriologist, a scientist who studies germs. He was experimenting in his laboratory at St. Mary's Hospital in London, England, and set one of the laboratory plates containing staphylococci bacteria beside an open window. Later, when he returned to the plate, he discovered some mold had blown in the window and contaminated the bacteria.

With the experiment "spoiled," many people would have thrown it away, but Fleming reexamined the plate. Under his microscope, he saw mold growing on the staphylococci. But around the mold there was a clear zone. The deadly staphylococci were actually being dissolved by the mold.

Through the accident of the moldy culture, Alexander Fleming gave the world penicillin.

Howard Florey, Ernst Chain, Norman Heatley, and other researchers at England's Oxford University experimented with Fleming's discovery and successfully developed penicillin into the lifesaving drug used all over the world today.

In 1945, Fleming, Florey, and Chain were awarded the Nobel Prize in medicine for their discovery and perfection of penicillin.

Today penicillin has affected almost every family in the developed nations. Doctors in the United States write over 80 million prescriptions for penicillin each year.

> **Andrew J. Moyer was inducted into the National Inventors Hall of Fame in 1987 for his Patents 2,442,141 and 2,443,989. Moyer's discovery of how to make penicillin in large quantities has saved millions of lives and prevented untold suffering from infectious diseases.**

X Rays

X ray machines are located in almost every hospital, dentist's office, and clinic in America. They are even in airport terminals where you can watch airport officials x-ray carry-on luggage.

Credit for the invention of X rays goes to Wilhelm C. Roentgen, who died in 1923. Roentgen was a German physicist and professor at the University of Würzburg. On November 8, 1895, he was working in his laboratory with a Crookes tube, a vacuum tube which produced streams of weak electrons called cathode rays. While experimenting in a darkened room with cathode rays and an electric current, he noticed that a fluorescent screen three or four feet away glowed. He was amazed since the Crookes tube was surrounded by black paper that prevented ordinary light from escaping. A popular story says he discovered the rays' penetrating power when he realized that he had unknowingly photographed a key which was inside a book.

Roentgen continued his experiments with the new invisible rays, and named them X rays since they were unknown. Later, some scientists called them Roentgen rays. Roentgen was awarded the Nobel Prize in physics in 1901 for his discovery of X rays.

A recent study reported that approximately 154 million Americans receive 312 million X rays each year. That amounts to approximately $12.5 billion spent on X rays in the United States annually. But more than just a medical discovery, X rays are also used in astronomy, chemical analysis, and industry.

— A person who receives too many X rays risks getting cancer, leukemia, cataracts, burns, or other health problems. Pregnant women are advised to avoid X rays, and all people should request that a "lead apron" be used to shield their eyes and reproductive organs during an X ray.

— The measure of doses of radiation produced by X rays is called a rad, a rem, or a roentgen.

— Radio waves have wavelengths of 12 inches to several miles. Visible light waves have wavelengths of about 20 millionths of an inch. X rays have wavelengths of about 4 billionths of an inch.

3

FUN, FUN, FUN

Someone once said, "Failure is the battle scar of someone who tried." But success can be that battle scar, too!

The Frisbee Disc

The Frisbee was invented 2,700 years ago.

Well . . . not really!

Discus throwing was a part of the early Olympic games in Greece 2,700 years ago. And the design of the Frisbee disc is similar to the discus thrown in the Olympic games. But the Frisbee is a Frisbee, not a discus. And its invention was *not* the result of some inventor staying up nights.

The original Frisbee was spelled Frisbie and it was metal. It was not invented to be thrown—except into an oven. It was a pie tin stamped with the words "Frisbie Pies" since the pies came from the Frisbie Bakery in Bridgeport, Connecticut.

The Frisbie pie tins would probably have done nothing more than hold pies if it hadn't been for some Yale University students. The Yale students bought Frisbie pies and once the pie was eaten, they began tossing the tins to each other. They would call out, "Frisbie!" to the person to whom they were tossing the pan, or to warn people walking nearby to watch for the flying objects.

And so, intending simply to toss a pie tin back and forth, the Yale University students invented what has grown into the Frisbee we know today.

Walter F. Morrison produced the first plastic models. The Wham-O Manufacturing Company of San Gabriel, California, began manufacturing Frisbee discs in the mid-1950s and since 1957 has made sixteen models. Now about thirty companies make flying discs.

There are flying disc clubs, tournaments, champions, a world association, and a publication just for flying disc enthusiasts. The National Frisbee Disc Festival is held each September.

The *Guinness Book of World Records* reports that the record time for keeping a flying disc aloft was set by Don Cain on May 26, 1984, when he kept one in the air for 16.72 seconds.

Disc play is good exercise. It's fun. It's easy, yet challenging. It doesn't cost much. And, best of all, it's a sport you can enjoy with your favorite dog!

Piggy Bank

Dogs bury bones.
Squirrels gather nuts to last through the winter.
Camels store food and water so they can travel many days across deserts.
But do pigs save anything? No! Pigs save nothing. They bury nothing. They store nothing.

So why do we save our coins in a piggy bank? The answer: Because someone made a mistake.

During the Middle Ages, in about the fifteenth century, metal was expensive and seldom used for household wares. Instead, dishes and pots were made of an economical clay called pygg.

Whenever housewives could save an extra coin, they dropped it into one of their clay jars. They called this their pygg bank or their pyggy bank.

Over the next two hundred to three hundred years, people forgot that "pygg" referred to the earthenware material. In the nineteenth century when English potters received requests for pyggy banks, they produced banks shaped like a pig. Of course, the pigs appealed to the customers and delighted children.

Pigs are still one of the most popular forms of coin banks sold in gift shops today.

- "Plutology" is the study of wealth.
- "Mammonism" is the greedy pursuit of riches.
- Piggy banks are helpful for persons with "peniaphobia," an abnormal fear of poverty.
- Cathy's mother took her to the bank to open her first bank account. "It's your account," the mother said, "so you fill out the application." Cathy was doing fine until she came to the space for "Name of your former bank." Cathy hesitated, then wrote, "Piggy."

Silly Putty

Sand.

There's lots of sand on Planet Earth. In fact, there's tons of it.

From sand, chemists can refine silicon. Plenty of silicon.

During World War II, the United States government needed a synthetic rubber for airplane tires, soldiers' boots, and other uses. Since silicon was so widely available, the government asked several large companies to have their engineers try to make a rubber substitute out of silicon.

In 1944 at General Electric, one of the engineers working on the silicon experiments was James Wright. One day while he was doing tests with silicon oil, he added boric acid. The result was a gooey substance that bounced.

Unfortunately, it had no apparent use. Samples were sent to engineers all over the world, but no one could find a use for it.

Then in 1949, four years after the war ended, a man named Peter Hodgson thought of an idea. After borrowing $147, he encased the goo in plastic "eggs" and renamed it "Silly Putty." Then he began selling it as a toy, first to adults and several years later to children.

It stretches. It bounces. When whacked with a hammer, it shatters. If it is pressed against newspaper comics, it will pick up the imprint. Silly Putty is truly amazing. It is now over forty years old, and was one of the first "fad" toys in America.

It has been used by athletes to strengthen their hand and forearm muscles. It can level the leg of a wiggly table or clean typewriter keys. It removes lint from clothes and animal hair from furniture.

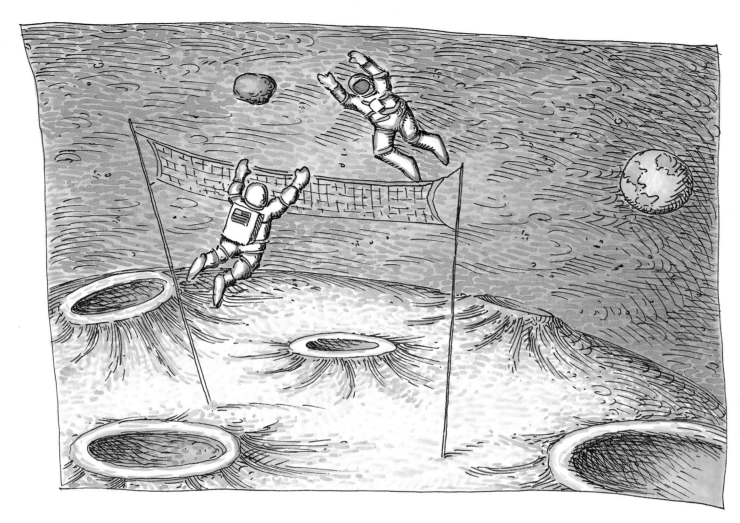

The astronauts on the *Apollo 8* spacecraft played with Silly Putty when they got bored, and they used it to keep tools from floating around after they left the Earth's gravity.

It was used by the Columbus Zoo in Ohio in 1981 to take hand and foot prints of gorillas.

It's the toy with only one moving part, and, best of all, Silly Putty is still priced so almost everyone can afford it.

Slinky

In 1943, during World War II, an engineer in the United States Navy was on a new ship's trial run. As he worked, a torsion spring suddenly fell to the floor. The spring flip-flopped as the ingenious man watched.

The naval engineer's name was Richard James, and when he returned home, he remembered the spring and the interesting way it flip-flopped. James and his wife Betty perfected a long steel ribbon tightly coiled into a spiral. They began production in 1945.

From that spring's accidental fall came a toy Americans have enjoyed for over forty years: the Slinky.

The nonelectrical, no-battery-required, nonvideo toy has fascinated three generations of children and adults alike. According to one estimate more than two million Slinkys have been sold and the only change in the original design has been to crimp the ends as a safety measure.

Betty James is now the company president and the Slinky is still hopping, skipping, jumping, and bouncing across floors and down stairs all over America.

4

ALL KINDS OF
ACCIDENTAL THINGS

William E. Gladstone once said, "No man ever became great or good except through many and great mistakes."

In 1875 the director of the United States Patent Office quit his job and suggested that his department be closed. There was nothing left to invent, he insisted.

Someone once asked, if necessity is the mother of invention, why does so much unnecessary stuff get invented? Among the more unusual patents granted in the United States are:

— a propeller-driven rocking chair
— an automatic spaghetti-spinning fork
— a power-operated pool cue stick
— a baby-patting machine
— an electronic snore depressor
— a parakeet diaper
— an alarm clock that squirts the sleeper's face

There is an Invention Convention in Philadelphia, Pennsylvania, on the first of April. The organizers say it is to "showcase inventors and present an inventor-of-the-year award."

Bricks

In New York City the Empire State Building was constructed with over 10 million bricks.

The Great Wall of China stretches fifteen hundred miles and contains almost 4 billion bricks.

Bricks have been used for nine thousand to ten thousand years, making them the oldest man-made building material.

Some archaeologists believe that the first bricks were made by accident. They were probably formed when mud or silt was deposited by the Nile River in Egypt. After the mud hardened into slabs, the slabs cracked. When an Egyptian walking along the Nile saw the slabs, he realized they could be shaped into blocks and used for building.

Some of the ancient bricks that have been found are as strong as the bricks manufactured today. The method of making bricks is still almost the same. Clay is mined, crushed, and mixed with water. The thick goo is then shaped, dried, and baked. Machines have made the crushing and mixing processes easier. Large ovens have replaced the sun drying. But the basic procedure has changed very little.

Brick plants are built near clay deposits suitable for brick making. One site is near the town of Malvern, Arkansas. Total production there is 150 million bricks a year—so many that Malvern is called the Brick Capital of the World. The town celebrates each year with a Brickfest.

There are even people who collect bricks. Their organization is called the International Brick Collectors Association. There, adults as well as children from the United States, Canada, Great Britain, New Zealand, and Australia share their interest in bricks. But they don't collect just any brick. They collect bricks that have names or markings on them.

Anyone interested in old bricks can visit the General Shale Museum of Ancient Brick, 3211 North Roan Street, Johnson City, Tennessee 37601. Among many fascinating bricks, a visitor can see:

— The oldest sun-dried brick ever found. It is from beneath the biblical city of Jericho. Experts estimate it is between nine thousand and ten thousand years old.

— The oldest fired brick ever found. It was discovered at Kalibangan, India, and is five thousand years old.
— A sixty-four-pound brick from a fortress of King Solomon.

This museum is free and open during standard business hours.

Glass

Bullets can bounce off it. Noise can shatter it. You can see through it or see yourself in it. It has gone into the oven, to the bottom of the ocean, and to the moon.

But we'll probably never know exactly who invented glass or when it was discovered. Perhaps workers noticed glass that accidentally resulted from a manufacturing process using fire.

Pliny the Elder, a first-century Roman writer, claims Phoenician sailors accidentally invented glass. He suggests the sailors were camping on the shores of Palestine and brought ashore two blocks of natron (carbonate of soda) from their ship's cargo. They used the blocks to support their cooking pots over the fire where they were camped. The fire caused the natron and the beach sand to melt together and create glass.

Historians know glass has been used for at least six thousand years. Egyptians were one of the first people to make glass on a large scale. Solid glass beads (usually blue!) have been found in Egyptian ruins dating before 2000 B.C.

While the basic process for making glass has not changed, modern technology has improved the procedure and the quality.

GLASSBLOWING

The art of glassblowing was not discovered until about the first century B.C. when a glassmaker's tube accidentally closed on one end. To remove the blob of glass, he blew into the tube from the other end. Instead of opening, the blob formed a bubble—and he had unintentionally invented glassblowing.

While the same principle is still used for glassblowing today, modern machines have improved its efficiency. A machine can blow approximately two thousand light bulbs in one minute—quite an improvement over the methods used two thousand years ago.

SAFETY GLASS

One day in 1903 Edouard Benedictus, a French chemist, accidentally knocked a glass flask to the floor of his laboratory. The glass shattered, but when Benedictus glanced down, he was amazed that the broken pieces still hung together in the shape of the flask.

Benedictus discovered that cellulose nitrate, a type of liquid plastic, had been

stored in the flask but had evaporated. After the flask broke, the glass fragments clung to the strong plastic film that had formed on the inside of the flask.

Soon after his discovery, Benedictus read a newspaper article about automobile accidents in Paris and the many injuries caused by broken windshield glass. Benedictus knew his nitrocellulose-coated glass had a practical use.

Automobile manufacturers, however, wanted to keep the cost of cars down and weren't interested in using such expensive glass. Besides, they only installed safety measures to prevent accidents—not to prevent injury.

When World War I started in 1914, manufacturers used Benedictus's safety glass for gas mask lenses. Soon after the war was over, safety glass had proven itself in military battles, so automobile companies began using it for car windshields.

— A glass museum is located at the Corning Glass Center on Route 17, Corning, New York 14831. There is an admission charge.
— "Crystallophobia" is the abnormal fear of glass.
— According to the *Guinness Book of World Records,* the thinnest glass is 0.00137 inch. It is made in West Germany and is used in electronic and medical equipment.
— "Glass" in other languages is:

French	verre	German	Glas
Italian	vetro	Turkish	cam
Russian	stekló	Arabic	zougag
Japanese	garasu	Swahili	kioo

Ivory Soap

Ivory Soap is 99 44/100 percent pure . . . and IT FLOATS!

Did it take years of experimenting to get that soap to float?

Not exactly. Ivory Soap floated by accident.

Two brothers, James and David Gamble, were partners in the Procter & Gamble Co., which manufactured soap. For four years they had been developing a formula for a high quality soap at an affordable price.

In January 1878, the brothers finally perfected the formula. They called it simply "White Soap," and began production.

Several months later the accident occurred.

A large batch of White Soap was mixing when a workman at the factory went to lunch and left the machinery running. When he returned, he found that air had been worked into the mixture. He decided not to discard the batch of soap because of such a small error, and he poured the soap into the frames. The soap hardened and it was cut, packaged, and shipped.

A few weeks later, letters began arriving at Procter & Gamble asking for more of the soap that floated. The workman's error had turned into a selling point!

Harley Procter came up with the name "Ivory" while listening to a Bible reading at church one morning in 1879.

Ivory Soap is over a hundred years old and still $99^{44}/_{100}$ percent pure. But best of all, it still floats!

— If Ivory Soap is $99^{44}/_{100}$ percent pure, what's in it that is $^{56}/_{100}$ percent impure? Here's the answer:

uncombined alkali	0.11%
carbonates	0.28%
mineral matter	0.17%

— Approximately 30 billion cakes of Ivory Soap have been manufactured.

Paper Towels

The Chinese invented paper about two thousand years ago, but it wasn't until the late 1800s that paper was made from wood pulp. After the discovery of this method, almost anything was made of paper:

clothes	outhouses	railroad wheels and rails	coffins
boats	a church	skating rink floors	a piano
watches	chimneys	false noses	washtubs
horseshoes	barrels	bathtubs	house insulation

And, of course, bathroom tissue (otherwise known as toilet paper).

In the early 1900s, Scott Paper Company, a large distributor of bathroom tissue, purchased large rolls of tissue paper and converted them into bathroom tissue.

In 1907 one of the paper suppliers sent a shipment of paper that had too much wrinkling and was too heavy. Arthur Scott didn't return the paper to the manufacturer. Although it was unsuitable for bathroom tissue, he knew it could be used.

He perforated the tissue so it could be dispensed in individual sheets. He called the sheets Sani Towels and sold them to railroad stations, hotels, schools, and business and industrial buildings. In 1931, he made the disposable towels available to American homes.

Today they come in "decorator colors" or "country designs." Some are big and tough; others are strong and absorbent. Some are soft; others, economical.

But the paper towels we use today are the result of a paper manufacturer's mistake.

Post-it Notes

By now everyone knows what Post-it brand notes are: They are those great little self-stick notepapers.

Most people have Post-it Notes. Most people use them. Most people love them.

But Post-it Notes were not a planned product. No one got the idea and then stayed up nights to invent it.

A man named Spencer Silver was working in the 3M research laboratories in 1970 trying to find a strong adhesive. Silver developed a new adhesive, but it was even weaker than what 3M already manufactured. It stuck to objects, but could easily be lifted off. It was superweak instead of superstrong.

No one knew what to do with the stuff, but Silver didn't discard it.

Then one Sunday four years later, another 3M scientist named Arthur Fry was singing in his church's choir. He used markers to keep his place in the hymnal, but they kept falling out of the book.

Remembering Silver's adhesive, Fry used some to coat his markers.

Success! With the weak adhesive, the markers stayed in place, yet lifted off without damaging the pages.

3M began distributing Post-it Notes nationwide in 1980—ten years after Silver developed the superweak adhesive. Today they are one of the most popular office products available.

Vulcanization of Rubber

Tires.
Shoe soles.
Baby bottle nipples.
Artificial cow hearts.
These and hundreds of other things are made of rubber.

Rubber is the tree sap that puts the bounce in a basketball, keeps river water out of fishermen's hip boots, and rolled a rock collecting cart across the moon.

But rubber isn't a new discovery. An ancient pictograph shows figures bouncing little rubber balls, and on Christopher Columbus's second trip to the New World, he saw boys playing with balls made from the hardened juice of a tree.

Central and South American natives, as well as Spanish and Portuguese explorers, made crude shoes and waterproofed clothing with the milky liquid of the wild rubber tree. But hot weather melted the substance, later named latex, into a gooey, smelly mess. And in cold weather, the rubber turned brittle and shattered like glass.

In 1770, Joseph Priestley, an English scientist, found that the gum of the tree rubbed out his writing mistakes. With that fantastic discovery, it was named "rubber."

Many people believed rubber should have more uses, and a man named Charles Goodyear tried mixing it with magnesium, turpentine, alcohol, slaked lime, nitric acid, and finally with sulphur. Then one day in early 1839 in Woburn, Massachusetts, Goodyear accidentally dropped a glob of the rubber-sulphur mixture on a hot kitchen stove. As he scraped up the mess, he realized the stove's intense heat had made the rubber firm and flexible. He tested it outside in the frigid winter air. The next morning the rubber was not brittle.

Goodyear had succeeded. He named the heating process "vulcanization" after Vulcan, the Roman god of fire.

In his autobiography, Charles Goodyear admitted the discovery was not the result of "scientific investigation." He wrote that he "carelessly brought [the mixture] in contact with a hot stove."

Because of Goodyear's determination—and an accident—rubber is one of the world's major industries. Goodyear was inducted into the National Inventors Hall of Fame in 1976 for his invention of the vulcanization process. But the discovery didn't make Charles Goodyear a rich man. When he died in 1860, he was two hundred thousand dollars in debt.

— **Visit the World of Rubber Exhibit at the Goodyear Tire and Rubber Company, 1201 East Market Street, Akron, Ohio 44316.**
— **According to the *Guinness Book of World Records,* the largest tires manufactured are 12 feet in diameter, weigh 12,500 pounds, and cost $74,000 each.**
— **Hundreds of vines, shrubs, and trees contain rubber, including dandelion, milkweed, and sagebrush. Most of these plants contain such small amounts of rubber that it's not cost-effective to extract it.**

Scotchgard

"Scotchgard" is the brand name of a fabric protector. Apply it to carpeting or a chair cover and dirt won't stick to the fabric.

Minor miracle. Right?

In the 1950s, researchers at 3M were working with fluorochemicals to use on aircraft. When some spilled on a researcher's tennis shoe, she found the chemical was almost impossible to remove. As time went on she noticed that as her tennis shoes got dirty from wear, the spot where the fluorochemical spilled remained clean.

Scotchgard wasn't the laboratory's goal that day, but today it is still keeping carpeting, furniture, clothing, car upholstery, and many other things stain-free.

5

WHERE IN THE WORLD?

Most explorers' discoveries were accidental, including the discovery of America. Christopher Columbus was searching for a new route to the Orient when he found land that he mistakenly named the West Indies.

> "Who never walks save where he sees
> Men's tracks, makes no discoveries."
>
> J. G. Holland

Bangor, Maine

Bangor is a city in Maine, the New England state at the northeastern tip of the United States. But Bangor was not always this city's name. In fact, Bangor was named by mistake!

In 1772, a settlement was established called Kenduskeag Plantation. By 1791, it had 576 residents. The village elders decided to petition the governing Massachusetts Legislature to incorporate the settlement so it would be considered a city.

The people of Kenduskeag Plantation selected Reverend Seth Noble to make the journey to apply for incorporation and have their city named Sunbury.

Reverend Noble, being a religious man, often sang beautiful hymns. He also indulged in alcoholic beverages. It is assumed that Reverend Noble was intoxicated when he arrived at the incorporation office because when he was asked the new name for the town, he began singing one of his favorite hymns, "Bangor."

The clerk entered "Bangor" on the official document and that is the name the city still uses today.

Were the townfolk angry?

History says they weren't. They knew their reverend had good intentions and they agreed it couldn't hurt to have their city named after a hymn.

Jellico, Tennessee

Jellico, Tennessee. At last count, there were 2,798 people living in Jellico—plus an assortment of dogs, cats, and birds.

Jellico, Tennessee. That's the town's name, but no one planned to name it that.

In 1795, a few people began settling in the area. Soon the settlement became known as Smithburg because there were so many Smiths living there. But as the community grew, the townspeople decided they needed a new name for their town. They chose the name Jericho, after the biblical city of the same name.

But no one looked up the spelling, and Jericho was spelled J-e-r-r-i-c-o.

Then the clerk who typed the charter of incorporation made a typographical error and spelled Jerrico as J-e-l-l-i-c-o.

And so it stands today: Jellico, Tennessee.

Leaning Tower of Pisa

In the year 1174, Bonnano Pisano, an Italian engineer, began work on a bell tower for the cathedral in Pisa, Italy. When Pisano started, he had no idea the bell tower would become a tourist attraction *and* one of the most famous structures in the world. Nor did he guess it would be famous because of a mistake.

58

The tower was to be 185 feet high. Construction started and three stories were completed.

Then the tower began to lean. The soil beneath the tower was soft and the ten-foot-thick foundation was not strong enough to support the weight.

Pisano tried to offset the lean by making the new stories slightly taller on the short side, but the extra building materials caused the tower to lean still further.

Construction was halted for almost a hundred years.

In 1275 construction began again. This time two stories were built out of line with the others, in an attempt to alter the center of gravity.

The tower was finally finished in the fourteenth century, but each year it leans 1.25 millimeters (about a quarter of an inch). It currently tilts 5 degrees or about 17 feet (5.2 meters).

In 1934 the Italian government pumped concrete under the base to try to correct the leaning, but the tilt increased. Architects are still searching for a solution.

While the town of Pisa enjoys the money tourists bring when they visit the Leaning Tower of Pisa, they fear someday their tower will lean too far and become the Toppled Tower of Pisa.

— **Vital statistics:**

cylindrical shape	**296 steps to the top**
7 levels of columns and arches	**constructed of white marble**
a smaller level on top	**184½ feet high**

— **The great astronomer, mathematician and physicist Galileo was born in Pisa. He performed some of his experiments concerning the speed of falling objects from the Leaning Tower of Pisa.**

Nome, Alaska

Alaska became the forty-ninth state in 1959, but it was more than a hundred years earlier that the city of Nome, Alaska, was named.

The name "Nome" does NOT honor a famous explorer or a brave hero or a wise president.

"Nome" is NOT a Spanish or French or German word for anything.

It is, instead, an accident.

In the 1850s, a British ship was charting the waters and shoreline around Alaska. An officer noted on the map he was charting that a point of land did not have a name. He wrote, "? Name" on the map, meaning "Unknown Name."

When the ship returned to England and the maps were recopied, another drafts-man thought the "?" was "C." (for "Cape") and that the "a" in "Name" was an "o." So the draftsman inserted Cape Nome as the name of the area.

While this story is generally accepted, some locals have another version of how Nome got its name. The second explanation says when English explorers asked an Eskimo the name of the cape, they were told in Eskimo, "Kn-no-me," which meant, "I don't know."

Whichever version one wants to believe, the area with the "unknown" name has grown and flourished as "Nome."

South Dakota: Jog in the Boundary

South Dakota is known for many things:

— Mount Rushmore, where four United States presidents' faces are carved in granite
— The Black Hills, a beautiful range of mountains
— The Badlands, where nature has carved exquisite sculptures in barren land

Even the geographical center of the United States is in South Dakota.

Only eight miles west of that geographical center, a man named Rollin J. Reeves made a mistake over a hundred years ago.

On June 6, 1877, Reeves, along with his survey party and troops from the Third Cavalry, began surveying the western boundary of what is now South Dakota. They were to follow the 104th meridian north.

Reeves and his men made excellent progress until after the middle of July when they received news of attacks by Sioux in the area. Only a year earlier, over two hun-

dred cavalrymen had died with General George Custer in the Battle of the Little Big-horn about 170 miles to the northwest. It is understandable that the survey party was nervous.

The surveyors retreated about twenty-five miles to Spearfish until more troops could be assigned. When they returned to their camp at the Belle Fourche, Reeves discovered his wagons had been ransacked and some of his records and equipment stolen.

The party continued north over the rolling hills. They finished the surveying on August 1, 1877.

It was not until 1885 when Daniel C. Major continued the survey line north from where Reeves finished that he discovered Reeves' marker was seven eighths of a mile too far west. The mistake was never corrected and even today the jog in the western border of South Dakota can be found on any map.

Considering the danger Reeves and his survey party faced, few historians would criticize the surveying error.

Today the country surrounding the jog in South Dakota's boundary is fenced grazing land. Grass, sagebrush, and cactus cover the prairie. No one really cares that Rollin Reeves and his survey party were seven eighths of a mile west of the 104th meridian.

The cattle and sheep that graze on the land around his mistake don't mind.

The antelope, skunks, weasels, coyotes, and mink that roam on the land don't care.

And the rattlesnakes, prairie dogs, and sage hens don't know the difference.

It was an accident that turned out okay.

— **Not all surveying mistakes turn out so well. Other surveying errors were made nearby along Wyoming's border. When those mistakes were corrected years later, corners were moved as much as half a mile. The resurveying caused hard feelings for the ranchers who lost land.**

6

WHAT THEY WEAR

"Only he who does nothing makes a mistake." French Proverb

Cinderella's Glass Slipper

Everyone knows Cinderella. She's the famous fairy tale star.

Poor Cinderella had to stay home and work while her stepsisters attended the Prince's ball. But Cinderella's Fairy Godmother suddenly appeared and transformed Cinderella's rags into a gown. The Fairy Godmother warned Cinderella that she had to leave the ball by midnight because her gown would turn back to rags at that hour.

Cinderella had a wonderful time at the ball and forgot the warning until the clock began to strike midnight. In her hurry to leave, Cinderella lost one of her glass slippers.

The Prince had fallen in love with Cinderella and searched for the maiden who could wear the slipper. When he found Cinderella, they married and lived happily ever after.

This fairy tale probably began in China. Over five hundred versions of Cinderella have been told in Europe alone. The version most of us know came from Charles Perrault's 1697 book. And that is where a mistake was made.

In earlier versions, Cinderella's slippers were made of fur. *Vair* is an old French word which means a type of fur. *Verre*, which is pronounced the same as *vair*, means glass.

It is believed that when Charles Perrault wrote the French version of Cinderella three hundred years ago, he confused *vair* for *verre*. And poor Cinderella has had to wear glass slippers ever since.

VELCRO

For thousands of years, man has walked through fields of weeds and arrived home with burrs stuck to his clothing. It's amazing no one took advantage of the problem until 1948.

George de Mestral, a Swiss engineer, returned from a walk one day in 1948 and found some cockleburs clinging to his cloth jacket. When de Mestral loosened them, he examined one under his microscope. The principle was simple. The cocklebur is a maze of thin strands with burrs (or hooks) on the ends that cling to fabrics or animal fur.

By the accident of the cockleburs sticking to his jacket, George de Mestral recognized the potential for a practical new fastener. It took eight years to experiment, develop, and perfect the invention, which consists of two strips of nylon fabric. One strip contains thousands of small hooks. The other strip contains small loops. When the two strips are pressed together, they form a strong bond.

"Hook-and-loop fastener" is what we call it today. VELCRO, the name de Mestral gave his product, is the brand most people in the United States know. It is strong, easily separated, lightweight, durable, and washable, comes in a variety of colors, and won't jam.

There are thousands of uses for hook-and-loop fasteners—on clothing, shoes, watch bands, or backpacks; around the house or garage; in automobiles, aircraft, parachutes, space suits, or space shuttles; to secure blood pressure cuffs and artificial heart chambers. The list is never-ending.

The only bad thing about hook-and-loop fasteners is the competition they give the snap, zipper, button, and shoelace industries!

Leotards

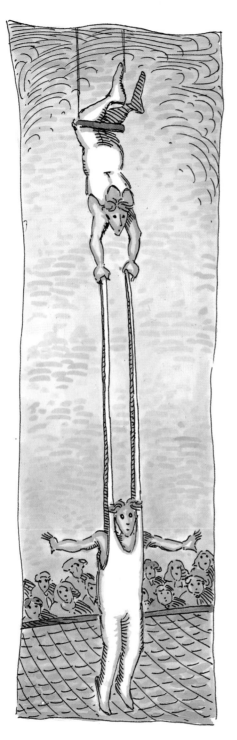

The dictionary says a leotard is "a one-piece, tight-fitting garment." Leotards are sometimes called "tights," and they are usually worn by gymnasts, acrobats, and dancers.

According to legend, Jules Léotard gave his name to the garment we now know as the leotard, but he didn't invent it.

A man named Nelson Hower was a bareback rider in the Buckley and Wicks Show in 1828. One day Hower's costume did not come back from the cleaners and he performed his act wearing his long underwear.

Other performers adapted the tight-fitting garments to their acts, but it took Jules Léotard to give it the name we know today.

Léotard, a French wire-walker and trapeze artist, began performing in Paris in 1859. He was the first acrobat to use a moving trapeze instead of a stationary bar. A song, "The Daring Young Man on the Flying Trapeze," was written about him.

Most people performing circus acts wore colorful, eye-catching costumes, but Jules Léotard chose the one-piece, tight-fitting garment. His performances were so outstanding that his name—and the "leotard" he wore—became famous.

- Today one of the most well-known persons to wear leotards is Superman!
- Visit the Circus World Museum, 426 Water Street, Baraboo, Wisconsin 53913, and the Ringling Circus Museum, 6255 North Tamiami Trail, Sarasota, Florida 33578.

Levi's Jeans

The invention of men's pants was certainly no accident.

And Levi Strauss's success at making what we now know as blue jeans was no accident either.

However, Levi Strauss did not leave New York in 1853 hoping to become the biggest and most successful blue jeans manufacturer in the world. He didn't even intend to manufacture blue jeans.

Levi Strauss went to San Francisco in 1853 intending to sell dry goods. The California Gold Rush of 1849 had attracted thousands of prospectors, and Levi planned to sell canvas for tents and Conestoga wagon covers. But as Levi Strauss talked to the prospectors, they told him, "Should'a brought pants. Pants don't wear worth a hoot in the diggin's!" Levi had a tailor make some pants from his brown canvas. Word quickly spread about the quality of "those pants of Levi's," or simply "Levi's jeans."

When his supply of canvas was gone, Levi switched to another sturdy fabric made in Nîmes, France. It was called *serge de Nîmes* (now known as denim). Levi improved his pants—changing the color to a deep blue and adding arcuate (arched) stitching and rivets to the pockets to prevent the weight of the gold nuggets from ripping them.

Levi Strauss's pants are still worn all over the world, and in 1976, a pair of Levi's jeans were put on display at the Smithsonian Institution in Washington, D.C., as part of the permanent American history collection.

— Why do we call them "jeans"? *Gene* was a form of the word *Genoese,* meaning from Genoa, Italy. In the late 1500s, sailors' pants were made of a cotton twill fabric made in Genoa. Those pants were often called *genes,* which was later changed to *jeans.*
— The average American college student owns five to six pairs of jeans.
— 425 million pairs of jeans are sold around the world each year.
— Of all the jeans sold in the United States, 21 percent are Levi's jeans.
— Americans spend $7 billion on jeans each year.

Trouser Cuffs

A story is told about the beginning of the cuff on men's trousers—that little roll-up on the pants leg near the ankle.

Supposedly, a large, formal wedding was being held in New York in the 1890s. A very fashionable Englishman was invited, but on the way to the church he was caught in a rainstorm. The man did not want to spoil his trousers, so he quickly rolled the bottoms up so they would not get wet.

Because of the storm, the Englishman was late, so he hurried into the church, forgetting to roll his pants legs down again.

Other guests noticed the rolled-up trousers, but didn't realize there was a real and practical reason for the cuffs. They thought the turnup was the latest in men's fashion.

The cuff quickly caught on in America, and quite by accident, the Englishman started a style that still reoccurs every few years in men's fashion.

THE NATIONAL INVENTORS HALL OF FAME

The National Inventors Hall of Fame was begun in 1973. According to the Patent and Trademark Office, the Hall of Fame "is dedicated to the individuals who conceived the great technological advances which this nation fosters through its patent system. The purpose of the Hall is to honor these inventors and bring public recognition to them and to their contributions to the nation's welfare."

Three things qualify a nominee for induction:

— coverage by a United States patent
— the contribution the invention has made to the nation's welfare
— the extent to which it promotes the progress of science and useful arts

On National Inventors Day in February, the Patent and Trademark Office in Arlington, Virginia, honors inventors selected to be inducted.

Thomas A. Edison was the first Hall of Fame inductee in 1973. (He received 1,093 patents during his lifetime.) Seventy persons have been added since 1973.

The public is invited to visit the National Inventors Hall of Fame. There is no admission charge and it is open during regular business hours. It is located at the Patent and Trademark Office, 2021 Jefferson Davis Highway, Arlington, Virginia. (The Hall will soon be moving to Akron, Ohio.)

There is a display for each inventor containing a brief description of his invention and an artifact connected with it.

SELECTED BIBLIOGRAPHY

The Amazing Story of Aspirin. London: Aspirin Foundation, 1981.

Bangor: History. Bangor, Maine: The Greater Bangor Chamber of Commerce.

Bergman, Peter M. *The Concise Dictionary of 26 Languages.* New York: New American Library, Signet, 1968.

Brasch, R. *How Did It Begin?* New York: David McKay Co., 1965.

Carter, Gordon. *Willing Walkers.* New York: Abelard-Schuman, 1965.

Charles Goodyear: 1800–1860 (biography). Akron, Ohio: Goodyear Tire and Rubber Co.

"Cinderella," *Encyclopaedia Britannica*, Vol. 3, 1986.

Clendinen, Barbara. "Avon Park Man Invents Brown and Serve Rolls," *Tampa Morning Tribune*, December 30, 1949, p. 4C.

Collier, James. "The Man Who Made a Million with Something Nobody Wanted," *Pageant*, April 1961, pp. 38–43.

d'Estaing, Valérie-Anne Giscard. *The World Almanac Book of Inventions.* New York: World Almanac Publications, 1985.

Everyone Knows His First Name. San Francisco: Levi Strauss & Co., 1986.

Facts/Things of Interest—Silly Putty. Easton, Pennsylvania: Binney & Smith.

Guinness Book of World Records, 1988 and *1989.* New York: Sterling Publishing Co., 1987 and 1988.

The History of Frisbee. San Gabriel, California: Wham-O.

"How a Dirty Sneaker Made Livingrooms Livable" (advertisement), *Newsweek,* April 21, 1986.

"In the Spirit of Ivory," *Ivory Soap—Celebrating 100 Years as America's Favorite.* Cincinnati, Ohio: The Procter & Gamble Co.

Jacobs, Francine. *Breakthrough: The True Story of Penicillin.* New York: Dodd, Mead & Co., 1985.

"Leaning Tower of Pisa," *Encyclopaedia Britannica,* Vol. 7, 1986.

McGrath, Molly Wade. *Top Sellers, USA.* New York: William Morrow & Co., 1983.

The Miracle of Rubber. Akron, Ohio: Goodyear Tire and Rubber Co., 1984.

"The Naming of Nome," *Nome, City of the Golden Beaches,* Vol. II, No. 1, Alaska Geographic Society, Alaska Northwest Publishing.

National Inventors Hall of Fame. Arlington, Virginia: U.S. Department of Commerce, 1988.

Nearing, Helen and Scott. *The Maple Sugar Book.* New York: Schocken Books, 1970.

"No Stopping," *The Philadelphia Inquirer,* October 3, 1984.

Perseverance, Patience Lead to Post-it Notes. St. Paul, Minnesota: 3M Co.

Polley, Jane. *Stories Behind Everyday Things.* Pleasantville, New York: The Reader's Digest Association, 1980.

Popsicle—A Part of American History. Englewood, New Jersey: Popsicle Industries, 1973.

"Potato Chips Rocketing Ahead," *PC/SFA 1985 Snack Food Management Report.* Alexandria, Virginia: The Potato Chip/Snack Food Association, July 1985.

Putnam, Peter Brock. *Love in the Lead.* New York: E.P. Dutton, 1979.

Refreshing Facts About Coca-Cola. Atlanta, Georgia: Coca-Cola Co., June 1987.

Robinson, Will G. "South Dakota Boundaries," *South Dakota Department of History, Report and Historical Collections,* Vol. 32. Pierre, South Dakota: State Historical Society, 1964.

Scott: The Story of Paper Towels. Philadelphia: Scott Paper Co.

Smith, David C. *History of Papermaking in the United States.* New York: Lockwood Publishing Co., 1971.

Tennessee—A Guide to the State. New York: The Viking Press, 1939.

The Versatile VELCRO Fastener and *The VELCRO Fastener Way.* Manchester, New Hampshire: VELCRO, USA, 1983.

Watters, Pat. *Coca-Cola—An Illustrated History.* Garden City, New York: Doubleday & Co., 1978.

Zettler, Howard G., *-Ologies & -Isms—A Thematic Dictionary.* Detroit: Gale Research Co., 1978.

INDEX